The Mojito

SEASIDE PUBLISHING

THE Mojito

Heather McPherson

SEASIDE PUBLISHING

Gainesville / Tallahassee / Tampa / Boca Raton
Pensacola / Orlando / Miami / Jacksonville / Ft. Myers / Sarasota

Illustrations for *The Mojito* were created by Spencer Pettit.

23 22 21 20 19 18   6 5 4 3 2 1

Library of Congress Control Number: 2017947803
ISBN 978-0-942084-87-0

SEASIDE PUBLISHING

Seaside Publishing is a division of the University Press of Florida.

For a complete list of Seaside books, please contact us
Seaside Publishing
15 Northwest 15th Street
Gainesville, FL 32611–2079
1–352-392-6867
1–800-226-3822
orders@upress.ufl.edu
www.seasidepublishing.com

To my husband, Spencer Pettit,
whose generous spirit and creativity
inspire me every day.
Cheers!

Contents

Introduction

Food historians love to quibble about a drink's origins, but most have accepted the Bacardi distillery's position: "The mojito either came from the Spanish word *mojar*, which means to wet, or the African word *mojo*, which means to cast a spell. Anybody who's ever tasted one will agree that it's thirst quenching and spellbinding in equal measures."

A precursor to the mojito may have been El Draque, a potent pour developed in the 1500s and named after Sir Francis Drake. The drink, more medicinal than the modern mojito, consisted of a primitive form of rum that likely had a moonshine kick and that was somewhat tempered by sugarcane juice, fresh lime juice, and mint.

Havana, Cuba, is the modern mojito's birthplace. The Bacardi company thrived there before political unrest led the family to flee to Puerto Rico. While Bacardi dominates the bar scene there, locals largely prefer their cocktails made with Don Q rum.

The mojito has several potent cousins. The caipirinha, Brazil's national cocktail, is made with cachaça, a sugarcane-based distilled spirit, sugar, and fresh lime. Planter's punch, a Jamaican beverage that evolved into a Carolina mainstay, includes rum, lime juice, sugar, and citrus juices (pineapple, orange, and grapefruit). And then there is the mint julep—the southern libation most often associated with the Kentucky Derby—which consists of bourbon, sugar, water, crushed or shaved ice, and fresh mint served in a silver cup or highball glass.

But the ingredients for a mojito are simple: top-notch rum, juicy lime wedges, fragrant mint leaves, extra-fine sugar, and a burst of effervescence from club soda. The variations bring complexity into play. Seasonal fruits and herbs, different rums, and creative ways to achieve the refreshing, bubbly finish are just a few of the ways this tropical treat has no bounds.

In addition, the mojito elements lend themselves to more than a bar menu. Sweet and savory dishes are enlivened by this easygoing combination of taste and textures. From glazes to marinades and ice cream to cakes, the mojito has made its mark on the culinary scene.

Cheers to the mojito, a time-honored beverage with a versatile flavor profile!

I

Libations and Light Elixirs

Before starting on our mojito journey there are techniques and elements key to all the cocktails: muddling, types of mint, and the choice of rums.

The Muddler

Muddling actually has a tool—the appropriately named "muddler." It's a sturdy device made from wood or metal. Wood muddlers are rounded on the ends like pestles used for crushing and grinding substances in a mortar. Metal muddlers have flat, round ends coated with rubber that give it an old-fashioned meat tenderizer look. But before you rush out to buy a new gadget, a wooden spoon works just as well.

As the root of the name implies, a muddler is used to mix together elements of recipes. But for classic mojitos, the tool is mainly needed to mash and tear the mint leaves so that the herb's essential oils are released.

The Mint

This perennial herb has many varieties with flavor nuances. Classic mojitos require spearmint, but peppermint, apple mint, chocolate mint, and orange mint varieties will shake up your flavor profiles.

In the garden or at the market, look for bright green, crisp leaves that show no signs of wilting or browning.

The Rum

Any liquor store's assortment of rum is a bewildering choice of clear to rich amber spirits. Classic mojitos call for white or light rum, but don't let that limit your imagination. Here's an overview:

- White: Also called light rum, it is distilled in white oak barrels then filtered to make it clear. White rum usually isn't aged, resulting in an uncomplex profile with subtle hints of vanilla.
- Golden: A spirit that has aged in amber oak barrels. The end result can have notes of toffee and banana.
- Dark: Aged in charred oak barrels, this elixir is sometimes called black rum. The robust distilled spirit is subtly smoky with caramel overtones.
- Spiced: Once an inexpensive way to mask poorly made liquor, today's spiced rums offer complex flavors with herbal hints, citrus fruits, and butterscotch finishes.

Mint Orange Agave Nonalcoholic Mojito

This recipe from the Florida Department of Citrus uses agave nectar, a naturally occurring sweetener that has a lower glycemic index value than other sweeteners. It is available at supermarkets and natural foods stores.

Yield: 1 serving

8 large fresh mint leaves
⅓ cup ice
½ cup freshly squeezed orange juice
2 tablespoons freshly squeezed lime juice
2 tablespoons agave nectar
¼ cup water

1. Place mint leaves in the bottom of a glass. With the back of a spoon, bruise mint to break up slightly to release flavor.
2. Add ice.
3. Combine all remaining ingredients, stir, and pour over mint and ice.

Recipe note: To add more minty flavor to this drink, mix ¼ cup sugar with 1 tablespoon chopped mint leaves. Stir. Pour onto plate. Wet rim of glass and dip into mixture prior to adding drink.

Bacardi Mojito

Raise a toast to the drink that started it all.

Yield: 1 serving

12 fresh spearmint leaves, plus sprig for garnish
½ lime, sliced
2 tablespoons simple syrup (equal amounts sugar and
    water heated until sugar dissolves, cooled)
Cubed ice
1½ ounces light rum
Club soda
Lime wedge

1. In a tall glass, muddle mint leaves and lime. Add simple
   syrup and fill the glass with ice.
2. Add rum and top up with club soda; stir well. Garnish
   with lime wedge and mint sprig.

Watermelon Mojito

Watermelon melded with fresh mint and lime juice come together in this toast to summer.

Yield: 1 to 2 servings

3 pieces of fresh mint, chopped
¼ cup watermelon puree (see note)
½ teaspoon grenadine syrup or pomegranate juice
3 tablespoons freshly squeezed lime juice
2 ounces light rum
Ice
Chilled sparkling water or club soda
1 or 2 sugarcane stirrers
1 or 2 lime wedges

1. With a muddler or wooden spoon, tear and smash the mint to coat the inside of a cocktail shaker. Add the watermelon puree, grenadine syrup, lime juice, and

rum. Shake vigorously and strain into a tall glass filled with ice.

2. Top up with sparkling water. Add sugarcane stirrer and lime wedge to each glass and serve.

How to make watermelon puree: Remove seeds from fresh watermelon and cut into large chunks. Put in a blender and process until smooth.

Spicy Mango Mojito

The richness of the mango nectar and spiced rum are great foils for the fiery pepper and potent mint leaves.

Yield: 1 to 2 servings

8 fresh mint leaves
3 lime wedges
1 jalapeño, sliced into wheels
Ice
1½ ounces spiced rum
2 tablespoons mango nectar
1 tablespoon extra-fine granulated sugar, or to taste
Club soda
Skewered whole jalapeño for garnish

1. In a cocktail shaker, muddle mint, lime wedges, and two jalapeño wheels together. Top with ice.
2. Add rum, mango nectar, and sugar. Shake vigorously. Strain and pour into a rocks glass and add club soda to fill. Stir. Lay skewered jalapeño across top of glass.

Blueberry Mojito

The refreshing pop of juicy blueberries offers a seasonal twist on a classic cocktail.

Yield: 1 serving

¼ cup fresh mint leaves
1 tablespoon freshly squeezed lime juice
1 teaspoon extra-fine sugar
4 tablespoons fresh blueberries
Ice
½ to ¾ cup lemonade, preferably homemade
Splash of club soda
1 ounce light rum
½ ounce dark rum
Mint sprigs and lime slices

1. In a tall 16-ounce glass, muddle mint leaves into lime juice and sugar. Add 2 tablespoons of the blueberries and mash until juicy.
2. Fill the glass three-quarters with ice. Add lemonade until the glass is two-thirds full. Add club soda, light rum, and remaining blueberries; stir. Slowly pour dark rum into the drink so it floats on top. Garnish with mint and lime.

Pineapple Mojito

Mojitos are generally low-alcohol choices. This tropical concoction packs a punch with 3 ounces of rum plus triple sec, an orange liqueur.

Yield: 1 serving

2 slices fresh pineapple
4 or 5 lime wedges
6 to 8 fresh mint leaves
Ice
3 ounces light rum
1 ounce triple sec
1 ounce fresh pineapple juice
Skewered pineapple and mint
Coarsely ground black pepper

1. Muddle pineapple, lime wedges, and mint in the bottom of a cocktail shaker.
2. Fill the shaker with ice and add rum, triple sec, and pineapple juice. Shake and strain into a tall glass filled with fresh ice. Lay the skewered pineapple across the top of the glass, lightly dust pineapple on skewer with pepper, and serve.

Passion Fruit Mojito

Passion fruit puree, found in the freezer section of most grocery stores, creates a tangy cocktail with sweetness and depth from the addition of dark brown sugar.

10 fresh mint leaves, plus sprig for garnish
1 lime, juiced, or to taste
1 teaspoon packed dark brown sugar, or to taste
Club soda
Crushed ice
1 ounce passion fruit puree
2½ ounces dark rum

1. Muddle mint leaves in the bottom of a cocktail shaker. Add lime juice, brown sugar, and a splash of club soda. Add ice, passion fruit puree, and rum. Shake vigorously and pour into a rocks glass. Garnish with a sprig of mint.

Recipe note: Adjust sugar and lime juice to taste.

Honey Ginger Mojito

Nature's natural sweetener mellows out the strong flavor of this ginger-laced cocktail.

Yield: 2 servings

10 fresh mint leaves, plus large leaves for garnish
1 slice peeled fresh ginger, about the size of quarter, plus
    thin slices for garnish
2 tablespoons orange blossom honey
2 tablespoons extra-fine sugar, or to taste
1 large lime, juiced
Ice
4 ounces spiced rum
4 ounces ginger ale, plus more as needed

1. Place mint leaves, ginger slice, honey, sugar, and lime juice in a cocktail shaker then muddle until sugar is dissolved and ginger and mint are crushed.
2. Add ice, rum, and ginger ale, then shake ingredients vigorously in the shaker. Strain into glasses filled with fresh ice. If needed, splash with additional ginger ale.
3. Skewer slices of ginger wrapped in large mint leaves for garnish.

Basil Lychee Mojito

Lychees, a tropical fruit native to China, are grown in Hawaii and Florida. The heart-shaped fruit is very sweet and has a subtle, perfumed taste. Lychee juice can be purchased in Asian food stores, and has no good substitutes.

Yield: 1 to 2 servings

1 large lime, quartered
1½ tablespoons palm sugar
½ cup fresh basil leaves
1 teaspoon simple syrup (equal
    amounts sugar and water heated
    until sugar dissolves, cooled)
3½ ounces lychee juice
3½ ounces golden rum
Ice
Skewered lychees

1. Put lime, palm sugar, and basil in a
   cocktail shaker. Muddle to infuse the flavors.
2. Add simple syrup, lychee juice, and
   rum. Fill the cocktail shaker with ice
   cubes and shake vigorously. Strain
   into rocks glasses over crushed ice.
   Garnish with skewered lychees.

Peach and Rosemary Mojito

Sweet and savory intermingle for this sophisticated cocktail. The pastel colors of the fruit and bright green of the chopped herb were made to play together.

Yield: 1 serving

1 large peach, pit removed and roughly chopped
1 ounce freshly squeezed lime juice
1 teaspoon finely chopped fresh rosemary
2½ ounces white rum
1 teaspoon simple syrup (equal amounts sugar and water
    heated until sugar dissolves, cooled)
Crushed ice
Club soda
1 sprig of rosemary

1. In cocktail shaker, muddle peach with lime juice and
   rosemary.
2. Add rum and simple syrup. Shake and pour (do not
   strain) over crushed ice in a tall glass. Top up with club
   soda. Place rosemary sprig across top of glass and use
   as a drink stirrer as well.

Carambola-Lemon-Thyme Mojito

Thyme gives the simple syrup a subtle savory flavor note in this cocktail that brings together the bright flavors of lemon and ripe carambola.

Yield: 6 to 8 servings

10 sprigs fresh thyme
2 lemons, sliced (use 2 slices in the simple syrup; see note), seeds removed
2 carambola, sliced (use 2 slices in the simple syrup; see note), any seeds removed
1 cup light rum
Carambola-lemon-thyme simple syrup (see note)
½ cup freshly squeezed lemon juice
Ice
Club soda

1. Combine thyme springs, lemon and carambola slices, rum, carambola-lemon-thyme simple syrup, and lemon juice in a tall pitcher. Muddle and stir all ingredients together.
3. Pour into glasses filled with ice and top up with club soda.

How to make carambola-lemon-thyme simple syrup: Combine 1 cup sugar, 1 cup water, 2 slices carambola, 2 slices lemon, ½

teaspoon freshly grated lemon zest, and 5 sprigs fresh thyme in a saucepan and stir on medium-low until it begins to bubble. Discard fruit and thyme springs and pour syrup into a glass container to cool completely.

Moonshine Lemonade Mojito

Artisanal moonshine has taken the once illegal homemade liquor to new heights. Sold in full-service fine wine and spirits stores, moonshine is as upscale as it gets—even down South.

Yield: 1 serving

5 fresh mint leaves, plus more for garnish (see note)
2 lemon wedges, plus slices for garnish
1 tablespoon extra-fine sugar
Shaved ice
1 ounce Ole Smoky Lemon Drop moonshine
1 ounce Ole Smoky White Lightnin' moonshine
Club soda
2 or 3 lemon drop candies

1. Muddle mint, lemon wedges, and sugar in a cocktail shaker.
2. Fill shaker with shaved ice and add both moonshines. Shake vigorously for 20 seconds and pour into a highball glass. Top up with club soda, add candies, and garnish with lemon slices and mint.

Recipe note: An alternative garnish is lemon balm, a mint cousin used in cooking and as a flavoring for the liqueurs Benedictine and Chartreuse.

Cranberry-Rosemary Mojito

This winter libation glistens with ruby jewel tones and sparkles with flecks of lemon zest. Make this drink by the pitcher for holiday parties. Herbs can be inconsistently potent. Feel free to adjust the minced rosemary to taste.

Yield: 1 serving

6 large fresh mint leaves
¼ teaspoon minced fresh rosemary
2 lime wedges
⅛ to ¼ teaspoon grated lemon zest
1½ ounces white rum
2 tablespoons low-sugar cranberry
    juice, or more to taste
1 heaping teaspoon whole berry
    cranberry sauce
Ice
Lemon-lime soda to taste (see note)
1 long sprig rosemary, leaves
    partially removed, to skewer
    with 4 or 5 fresh cranberries

1. Muddle mint, rosemary, lime wedges, and lemon zest in the bottom of a cocktail shaker.

2. Add rum, cranberry juice, and cranberry sauce. Shake vigorously and pour over ice.
3. Top up with lemon-lime soda to taste and garnish with the rosemary sprig skewer with cranberries.

Recipe note: Substitute a cranberry-flavored lemon-lime soda if desired.

Orange Tarragon Mojito

Flavor-infused rums add a splash of creativity to all kinds of libations—especially mojitos. Be judicious when using fresh herbs and citrus zest. They pack a wallop of flavor and the goal is to subtly enhance, not overpower.

Yield: 1 serving

5 large mint leaves, plus sprig for garnish
3 lime wedges
⅛ teaspoon grated orange zest
⅛ teaspoon minced fresh tarragon, plus sprig for garnish
2 teaspoons extra-fine sugar
2 ounces orange-flavored rum, such as Cruzan
Ice
Orange peel
1½ ounces club soda

1. Muddle mint, lime wedges, orange zest, tarragon, and sugar in a cocktail shaker.
2. Add rum and fill with ice. Shake vigorously.
3. Fill a cocktail glass with ice. Rub the rim with orange peel. Slap tarragon and mint stems against the back of your hand to release aromas. Strain rum mixture into glass. Top up with club soda. Garnish with mint and tarragon sprigs and orange peel.

Blackberry Mojito

In this recipe, the blackberries are gently crushed with the sugar, mint, and citrus juices. Pulverizing them would release the fruit's astringent tannins.

Yield: 1 serving

4 teaspoons extra-fine sugar
12 blackberries, plus more for garnish
8 large fresh mint leaves, plus sprig for garnish
1 tablespoon freshly squeezed lemon juice
1 tablespoon freshly squeezed lime juice
½ cup club soda
2 ounce spiced rum
Ice
Lemon peel

1. In a cocktail shaker, gently muddle sugar, berries, mint, and lemon and lime juices until berries are slightly broken down but not pulverized.
2. Add club soda and rum. Shake vigorously and serve over ice. Garnish with additional berries, mint sprig, and lemon peel.

Hot Mojito Tea

With tropical roots, mojitos are most associated with warm-weather indulging. But the flavor profile also works well in beverages that warm us up on cool nights.

Yield: 2 servings

6 fresh mint leaves
1 teaspoon brown sugar
1 English Breakfast tea bag
2 cups boiling water
2 ounces dark rum
Fresh lime wedges and Demerara sugar cubes

1. Rinse a small teapot with hot water. Add mint, brown sugar, tea bag, and boiling water; cover and let stand for 2 minutes.
2. Swirl tea bag throughout the pot, then press to release liquid trapped inside bag into mint mixture. Discard bag and stir in rum.
3. Strain into clear tea or coffee cups. Serve with lime wedges and Demerara sugar cubes.

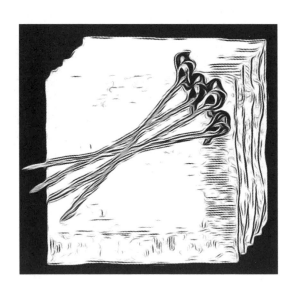

2

Savory Sensations

The flavor profile of the mojito easily crosses culinary lines into savory dishes. But the ingredients often need to be used differently and selected carefully. Take mint, for example: In general, the spearmint variety is used for drinks, but there are dozens of other types of this leafy green to use in other recipes. Here's a quick guide to common home garden and farm market varieties and how to use them.

- Spearmint: Use in marinades for lamb and game meats.
- Peppermint: The most intensely flavored member of the mint family lends itself well to adding flavor when steaming peas, carrots, and other vegetables. Add torn leaves to the water to let the essential oils escape into the liquid as it heats.
- Apple: With the scent of Granny Smith apples, these leaves can be julienned and tossed into salads and slaws.
- Pineapple: A mild mint with variegated foliage, this variety is highly aromatic, with sweet tropical notes and a minty citrus finish. Use to flavor fish, seafood, chicken, and pork.

- Orange: The notes of citrus mingle with spice and lavender undertones, making it a great match for pepper jellies, homemade vinegars, teas, salsas, salads, and sauces.

Mojito Grilled Shrimp Salad

The key flavor elements of a refreshing mojito cocktail are used to enliven grilled shrimp in this summer salad. The mint-, rum-, and lime-laced dressing can be used on fruit salad as well or to flavor grilled chicken or fish.

Yield: 4 servings

1 pound peeled and deveined large shrimp (about 36)
Coarse salt and pepper to taste
3 teaspoons extra-virgin olive oil
2 tablespoons freshly squeezed lime juice
2 tablespoons light rum or freshly squeezed orange juice
1 tablespoon chopped fresh mint
1 teaspoon extra-fine sugar
8 cups baby arugula
1 ripe Florida avocado, peeled and thinly sliced
1 large Florida mango, peeled and thinly sliced
½ cup sliced sweet onion

1. Preheat grill to 350 to 400°F (medium-high).
2. Combine shrimp, salt and pepper, and 1 teaspoon oil in a medium bowl. Thread 6 shrimp onto each of 6 (10-inch) skewers. Grill shrimp for 2 minutes on each side or until done. Remove shrimp from skewers.
3. Whisk remaining 2 teaspoons oil,

lime juice, rum or orange juice, mint, and sugar in a small bowl.

4. Arrange 2 cups of arugula on each of 4 plates. Top evenly with shrimp, avocado, mango, and onion. Drizzle with dressing.

Orange-Mojito Florida Lobster

The earthiness of the dried spices temper the sweetness of shellfish and tang of the vibrant zest. The seasoned butter can be frozen and used to flavor other shellfish including rock shrimp. The blend is also suitable for topping grilled beef.

Yield: 4 servings

For seasoned butter:
1 teaspoon cumin seeds, or to taste
½ teaspoon pink peppercorns, or to taste
½ teaspoon fennel seeds
1 stick unsalted butter
1 teaspoon grated orange zest
1 teaspoon chopped fresh thyme
½ teaspoon coarse salt, or to taste

4 (6- to 9-ounce) spiny lobster tails, split open in the shell
2 teaspoons fresh orange juice
Chopped fresh mint
Tendrils of orange peel

1. Make seasoned butter: In a small skillet, lightly toast cumin, peppercorns, and fennel. Let cool completely, then grind and crush with a mortar and pestle or coffee grinder. Combine ground spices with butter, orange zest, thyme, and salt. Scrape out onto parchment paper and form into a log. Wrap, twisting

the ends, and set aside in the refrigerator until ready to broil lobsters. Slice 4 medallions of the butter and let each soften.

2. Preheat oven broiler on medium-high. Place lobsters on a rimmed baking pan and make sure they are open down the middle. Evenly spread softened butter over the lobster tails' meat. Place lobsters in the oven on the middle rack under the broiler. Cook 5 to 7 minutes, until just barely cooked throughout. Remove lobsters from oven and let cool slightly.

3. Serve lobster tails warm, each drizzled with ½ teaspoon orange juice and garnished with mint and orange peel.

Recipe note: Substitute tangerine juice for the orange juice if desired.

Mojito Grilled Fish Tacos with Mango Salsa

Mangos have a not-so-subtle rum flavor profile. Using the super-sweet fruit in the salsa tames the fire from these jalapeño-infused tacos.

Yield: 4 servings

For mango-avocado salsa:
1¼ cups diced fresh Florida mangos
½ cup diced Florida avocado
1 jalapeño, seeded and minced
½ cup chopped red onion, or to taste
3 tablespoons fresh lime juice
½ cup freshly chopped flat-leaf parsley
Coarse salt and freshly ground pepper to taste

For marinade:
2 tablespoons olive oil
1 lime, zested and juiced
3 tablespoons spiced rum
1 jalapeño, seeded and minced
1 clove garlic, chopped
1 large shallot (or 2 small), thinly sliced
½ cup fresh mint leaves, chopped
1 cup flat-leaf parsley, chopped
1 teaspoon fennel seeds, toasted and ground
Coarse salt and freshly ground pepper to taste

1 pound white fish such as sheepshead or snapper
8 (4-inch) corn tortillas, warmed

8 lime wedges
1¼ cups crumbled cojita or feta cheese
Chopped fresh flat-leaf parsley
Hot sauce

1. For salsa, combine all ingredients and refrigerate, covered, until ready to serve.
2. For marinade, combine all ingredients. Add fish and marinate for 10 to 20 minutes.
3. Grill fish over medium-high heat until cooked, 4 to 6 minutes per side. The fish will be cooked when it flakes easily and is no longer translucent. Flake and cut the fish into one-bite pieces. Serve in tortillas spritzed with lime and topped with salsa, cheese, parsley, and hot sauce.

Baked Strawberry Mojito Ham

The holiday ham has earned its time-honored centerpiece position on the table probably because it is so easy to prepare. Glazes are an easy way to add your favorite flavor profiles to the smoky, savory flavor of pork.

Yield: 10 to 12 servings, with leftovers

1 (10- to 14-pound) spiral-sliced, fully cooked smoked ham

For glaze:
1 (12-ounce) can or bottle lemon-lime soda
¼ cup chopped fresh mint
1 tablespoon orange juice concentrate, thawed
¼ cup low-sodium soy sauce
1 cup strawberry jam
½ teaspoon freshly grated nutmeg
¼ teaspoon ground cloves

Sliced Florida strawberries

1. Heat oven to 325°F. Place ham on
   rack in roasting pan. Bake ham 30
   minutes.
2. Meanwhile, for glaze, whisk soda,
   mint, orange juice concentrate, soy
   sauce, jam, nutmeg, and cloves; set
   aside.

3. Pour half of the glaze on top of ham. Bake until ham is heated through, about 2½ hours or 15 to 18 minutes per pound. Remove from oven and drizzle with remaining glaze. Garnish with strawberries.

Mojito Marinated Pork Tenderloin with Roasted Pineapple Chutney

The tenderloin comes from the full pork loin. As the name indicates, the tenderloin is one of the most tender cuts of pork. Pork tenderloin makes an elegant entrée for a small dinner party but also can be roasted or grilled whole for a quick weeknight dinner. This recipe was developed by Michaela Rosenthal for the National Pork Board's America's Favorite Family Recipes Contest in celebration of National Eat Dinner Together Week.

Yield: 4 servings

1¼ pounds pork tenderloin (this may be two pieces)
Coarse salt and freshly ground pepper to taste

For marinade:
1 cup freshly squeezed orange juice
⅓ cup packed brown sugar
¼ cup extra-virgin olive oil
¼ cup finely chopped fresh mint
½ teaspoon ground cinnamon
½ teaspoon dry mustard

For chutney:
4 slices fresh pineapple, cut ½-inch thick
2 tablespoons butter, melted
2 tablespoons brown sugar

⅓ cup golden raisins
1 tablespoon dark rum
2 tablespoons freshly squeezed orange juice
¼ cup chopped sweet onion
2 teaspoons chopped fresh mint
Coarse salt to taste

Fresh mint sprigs
Steamed aromatic rice, such as jasmine or basmati

1. Season tenderloin with salt and pepper and place
   in a glass baking dish. Whisk together all marinade
   ingredients and cover tenderloin with marinade.
   Marinate in the refrigerator for 1 to 2 hours, turning
   pork occasionally. Remove pork from marinade
   (discarding excess).
2. Meanwhile, preheat broiler. For chutney, place
   pineapple slices on a parchment-lined baking sheet.
   Mix together melted butter and brown sugar; brush
   half of butter mixture onto top surfaces of pineapple
   slices. Broil for 2 minutes. Turn pineapple slices over
   and brush with remaining butter mixture. Broil for 1
   to 2 minutes more or until slightly softened. When
   pineapple has cooled, remove and discard peel and
   core; dice finely.
3. Heat oven to 350°F. In a large, heavy oven-safe skillet,
   sear pork over medium-high heat for 2 to 3 minutes
   or until all sides are lightly brown. Roast tenderloin in
   skillet, uncovered, in oven for 20 to 27 minutes, until

the internal temperature reaches 145°F. Let pork sit at room temperature for 5 to 10 minutes before cutting into 1½-inch-thick slices.

4. Meanwhile, plump raisins in rum and orange juice in a saucepan over low heat for 5 minutes. Remove from heat, add pineapple and remaining chutney ingredients, and stir to combine.

5. To serve, arrange pork (slices overlapping) on a heated serving platter and spoon chutney down the center. Garnish with mint sprigs and serve with rice.

Baked Tangerine Mojito Chicken Wings

Tangerine juice has a more concentrated flavor than orange juice. Use it when you are looking for a more pronounced flavor in a citrus-laced recipe.

For marinade:
¼ cup freshly squeezed tangerine juice
½ (12-ounce) can or bottle lemon-lime soda (use remaining soda in glaze; see below)
1 teaspoon minced tangerine peel
1 teaspoon grated lime zest
1 teaspoon minced garlic
¼ cup chopped fresh mint
¼ cup dark rum
2 tablespoons orange blossom honey
Coarse salt and freshly ground pepper to taste

3 pounds chicken wings, completely thawed if frozen

For glaze:
½ cup dark rum
½ cup chicken broth
½ (12-ounce) can or bottle lemon-lime soda
1 tablespoon packed light brown sugar

Garnishes: Sliced green onions, grated lime zest, and grated tangerine peel

1. In a large glass bowl or baking dish, combine marinade ingredients. Add chicken wings, tossing to coat. Cover with plastic wrap and refrigerate for 1 hour, tossing at least twice during that time.
2. Heat oven to 450°F. Discard marinade. Place chicken wings in a single layer on a rimmed baking pan lined with nonstick foil. Bake for 20 minutes.
3. While chicken wings are baking, combine glaze ingredients in a small saucepan. Simmer and stir until heated through and sugar is completely dissolved. Let cook until mixture thickens to coat the back of a spoon and glistens.
4. Remove wings from oven and lower temperature to 350°F. Generously brush wings on both sides with glaze. Return to the oven and bake for another 10 minutes.
5. Turn the oven to broil and broil for 8 minutes, flipping at the halfway mark so that both sides of the wings are crisp and the sauce becomes syrupy. Watch closely during the last 8 minutes so that wings do not burn.
6. Garnish wings with green onions and lime and tangerine zests.

Grapefruit Mojito Chicken Thighs

Chicken thighs are a juicy and flavorful alternative to chicken breasts. Marinated and topped with a citrus salsa, this dish makes for an easy weeknight meal. Brown rice and a fresh side salad complete the menu.

Yield: 4 servings

2 large red grapefruit (1 juiced, 1 sectioned and chopped)
2 large limes (1 juiced, 1 sectioned and chopped)
½ cup extra-virgin olive oil
1 tablespoon plus 1 teaspoon chopped fresh thyme
2 tablespoons chopped fresh mint
Coarse salt and freshly ground pepper to taste
1½ pounds skinless, boneless chicken thighs
¼ cup sliced green onions

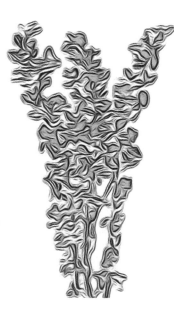

1. Combine citrus juices with ¼ cup oil, 1 tablespoon thyme, and 1 tablespoon mint and season with salt and pepper. Add chicken and toss to coat. Refrigerate for 15 minutes.
2. Combine chopped citrus in a glass bowl and fold in remaining oil, thyme, and mint. Add green onions.

Season lightly with salt and pepper. Set aside at room temperature to let flavors meld.

3. Remove chicken from refrigerator and let rest on the counter for 5 minutes to lose the chill. Discard marinade and grill the chicken thighs over medium-high heat, turning them occasionally, until they are lightly charred outside and cooked through, 8 to 10 minutes. Serve with the grapefruit and lime topping.

Recipe note: If desired, sweeten the grapefruit and lime topping with pinch of Florida raw sugar or a splash of lemon-lime soda.

Mojito Marinated Chicken

Chicken is a wonderful blank canvas. Cooked right, it has a juicy, clean flavor that needs little embellishment. Fresh herbs, citrus, and a distilled spirit dress turn plain chicken breasts into tropical dynamos.

Yield: 6 servings

¾ cup fresh lime juice
½ cup plus 2 tablespoons spiced rum
½ cup chopped fresh mint, plus sprigs for garnish
6 tablespoons mint syrup (see note)
1 tablespoon olive oil
Coarse salt to taste
6 chicken breast halves
3 large limes, quartered

1. Whisk lime juice, ½ cup rum, mint, mint syrup, oil, and salt together. Place chicken in a sealable plastic bag. Pour marinade over; seal bag. Turn bag and massage to distribute marinade. Refrigerate for 4 hours, turning bag twice.
2. Place lime quarters in a shallow bowl. Pour remaining 2 tablespoons rum over, tossing to coat. Let stand at room temperature.
3. Grill chicken until cooked through, about 15 minutes per side. Transfer to serving platter.

4. Grill limes until soft and lightly charred, about 5 minutes. Garnish platter with mint. Squeeze grilled limes over chicken and serve.

How to make mint syrup: Chop fresh mint leaves to make 1½ cups, packed. In a saucepan, bring 1 cup extra-fine sugar, 1 cup water, and mint to a boil, stirring until sugar is completely dissolved. Simmer syrup for 2 minutes. Strain through a fine sieve, pressing hard on the caught leaves with the back of a spoon. Cool mixture completely.

Duck Breast Mojito Empanadas

This great party fare was inspired by Maple Leaf Farms, which supplies duck meat to mainstream supermarkets and restaurants throughout the nation. The fresh salsa explodes on the palate with citrus and fresh herbs.

Yield: 20 servings

3 (7½-ounce) packages Maple Leaf Farms duck breast
20 (⅛-inch-thick) round plantain slices
8 ounces Monterey Jack cheese, shredded
2 bunches green onions, thinly sliced
20 (2-ounce) dough rounds, cut from ready-to-use pie crust pastry
2 large eggs, lightly beaten
4 teaspoons water

For mojito salsa verde:
1 cup rum
¼ cup sugar
¼ cup honey
1 jalapeño, seeded and minced
¼ teaspoon chile flakes
4 limes, zested and juiced
2 lemons, zested and juiced
2 cups fresh mint leaves, coarsely chopped
1 bunch green onions, coarsely chopped
1 cup chopped fresh cilantro
3 garlic cloves, minced
1 large shallot, minced

1. Prepare duck breasts according to package directions. Cool and slice thinly.
2. Heat oven to 375°F.
3. Layer duck breast, plantains, cheese, and green onions on one side of each pastry round. Moisten edges of pastry with water; fold side with filling almost to the opposite side, allowing opposite pastry edge to extend ⅛ inch. Curl the extension over the top, then press gently to seal. Crimp with a fork.
4. Make egg wash by mixing eggs with water. Brush egg wash onto empanadas. Pierce each empanada once with fork. Bake for 10 minutes, or until golden brown.
5. For salsa, combine rum, sugar, and honey in a saucepan. Over medium-low heat, bring to a boil. Add remaining ingredients and bring back to a boil, stirring occasionally. Serve at room temperature with warm empanadas.

Mojito-Garlic Lamb Chops

The sauce in this recipe amps up the flavor by melding rum, pineapple juice, and butter with all the flavorful browned bits from the cooking pan.

Yield: 4 servings

8 rib lamb chops
1 tablespoon olive oil
Coarse salt and freshly ground pepper to taste
1 teaspoon garlic powder
1½ teaspoons grated lime zest
Cooked quinoa
Freshly squeezed lime juice
¼ cup rum
¾ cup pineapple juice
2 tablespoons unsalted butter
Torn fresh mint leaves

1. Heat a large nonstick skillet over medium-high heat. Brush chops with oil. Combine salt and pepper, garlic powder, and lime zest. Sprinkle seasoning evenly over lamb. Cook chops for 2 to 3 minutes per side for medium-rare. Arrange chops on top of a mound of cooked quinoa and drizzle meat lightly with lime juice.
2. Deglaze skillet with rum (being careful not to flame liquid), then add pineapple juice and boil until reduced by half, scraping any browned bits from the bottom of the pan. Remove from the heat. Stir in butter. Spoon sauce over chops. Garnish with mint.

Mojito Strip Steak

This beef dish is similar to a chimichurri-style steak. In this recipe, the mint steps in for the parsley for a refreshing turn.

Yield: 4 servings

½ teaspoon grated lime zest
3 tablespoons freshly squeezed lime juice
¼ cup chopped fresh mint
2 to 3 tablespoons light rum
2 (½-inch-thick) beef strip steaks, trimmed and cut in half
    crosswise (about 1 pound)

For pico de gallo:
2 cups chopped seeded tomato (2 medium)
⅓ cup chopped red onion
⅓ cup chopped fresh mint
2 tablespoons freshly squeezed lime juice
1 jalapeño, seeded and chopped
Coarse salt and freshly ground pepper to taste

1. Combine lime zest, lime juice, mint, and rum in a
   large resealable plastic bag. Add steak to bag and
   seal. Marinate in refrigerator for 30 minutes, turning
   occasionally.
2. While steak marinates, combine pico de gallo
   ingredients. Set aside to let flavors meld.
3. Prepare grill. Remove steaks from marinade,

discarding marinade. Season steaks with salt and pepper. Place steaks on a grill rack coated with cooking spray. Grill for 2 minutes on each side or until desired degree of doneness. Let stand for 3 minutes. Cut steak into slices. Serve with pico de gallo.

3

Delightful Desserts

The treats in this chapter run the gamut from frozen pops to warm baked goods. They are simply suggested road maps to satisfy a craving for something sweet. The recipes can be easily adapted to personal preference.

But before we indulge, let's pause for a little refresher on the light and airy quality of the mojito that can be found in sugar-kissed meringues—toppings and foundations that can make so many desserts so irresistible.

Meringue

Meringues are simply a soft or stiff foam of beaten egg whites and sugar. The most critical factor in making meringue is humidity. Because it has a high sugar content, meringue can absorb moisture from the air and become limp and sticky.

What the cook needs to know:

- Beaters and bowls must be clean and completely free of fat or oils. Glass and metal vessels work best.
- After separating eggs, allow the whites to come to room temperature. This will enable them to reach the fullest volume.

- Beat the whites with cream of tartar (⅛ teaspoon for each 2 egg whites) until foamy. Cream of tartar, a byproduct of winemaking, lends stability to egg foams.
- Add extra-fine sugar and extracts to sweeten and flavor after the whites just begin to turn foamy. The fine sugar dissolves more easily than regular sugar, preventing gritty meringues.

Type of Meringues

The differences are in the ratio of egg whites to sugar, the method of mixing, and the method of cooking.

- Soft: Used to top pies and puddings. The usual ingredient ratio is 2 tablespoons sugar to each 1 egg white. Beat the meringue until soft peaks form, then swirl it over a hot, precooked pie filling or pudding. Sometimes, after baking, liquid accumulates between the meringue and the filling. You can minimize this weeping if the filling is hot when you put the meringue on it. To keep a pie meringue from shrinking during baking, make sure the meringue touches the edge of the crust or the dish all around. A meringue made from 3 egg whites will cover a 9-inch pie.
- Hard: Used as a foundation for fruit and pudding fillings. The usual ingredient ratio is 4 tablespoons sugar to each 1 egg white. Beat until stiff peaks form.
  You can bake a meringue on a baking sheet lined with foil or parchment. Depending on how you intend to use a hard meringue, you can pipe it with a pastry

bag and tip, shape it gently with a spoon or spatula, or bake it in a greased pie plate, cake pan, or springform pan. Meringue baked in a pie plate forms a delicate crust for fillings, such as chocolate or lemon, and the result is often known as angel pie. Meringue baked in a cake pan or springform pan is often served with whipped cream and fruit and is called a pavlova. Bake in a preheated 225°F oven for 1 to 1½ hours, then turn off the heat and continue to dry the meringues for at least another hour in the oven. When done, hard meringues should be white, dry, and crisp.

- Italian: Also known as boiled frosting, this meringue is used to finish cakes or to create a base for frozen desserts. When folded into whipped cream, Italian meringue becomes chantilly meringue. To make Italian meringue, beat hot sugar syrup into beaten egg whites.

- Poached: Also called snow eggs or oeufs à la neige, these are often served with custard or fruit sauce. Poached meringues are also the islands in a "floating island" pudding. To make, drop soft, hard, or Italian meringue mixture by spoonfuls onto simmering whole milk. Cook, uncovered, until firm, about 5 minutes. You don't need to turn over small spoonfuls, but larger ones may require turning halfway through the cooking time. Remove the poached puffs with a slotted spoon and drain them on absorbent paper. Chill before serving.

Mint Meringue Kisses

Always make meringue on dry days. These Mint Meringue Kisses can absorb moisture from the air, causing them to flatten out when baked and to lose their crispness. To re-crisp: If stored kisses lose their crispness, bake in 200°F oven 15 to 20 minutes. To store, place meringue kisses in tightly sealed container, with waxed paper between layers.

Yield: about 60 kisses

4 large egg whites, at room temperature
½ teaspoon cream of tartar
1¾ cups powdered sugar, sifted
1 cup crushed green-and-white spearmint candies, plus
    more for garnish
Freshly grated nutmeg

1. Heat oven to 225°F.
2. Beat egg whites and cream of tartar in mixer bowl with whisk attachment on high speed until foamy. Beating constantly, add powdered sugar, 2 tablespoons at a time, until whites are glossy and stand in stiff peaks.
3. Fold in crushed candies. Spoon into pastry bag fitted with large fluted or plain tip. Pipe meringue onto baking sheets lined with parchment paper. (Alternatively, you can use a tablespoon to dollop mounds onto the parchment.) Sprinkle with additional crushed candies and lightly dust with nutmeg.

4. Bake until firm, about 1 hour. Turn off oven. Let dry in oven, with door closed, until cool and crisp, at least 1 hour.

Recipe note: One cup extra-fine granulated sugar can be substituted for the powdered sugar. Beat after each addition until sugar is dissolved before adding the next. Rub a bit of meringue between thumb and forefinger; it should feel completely smooth.

Variations:

Go Nuts: Meringue kisses can be made with walnuts, pistachios, almonds, or macadamias instead of the candies.

Chocolate Mojito: Sprinkle with chocolate jimmies before baking.

Zest for Life: Add citrus zest to whipped egg whites for additional flavor.

Mojito Bars

Wow the guests crowding the dessert bar at your next potluck party with these sweet and tangy treats.

Yield: 15 to 18 small bars

3 tablespoons light rum
16 fresh mint leaves, chopped
¾ cup unsalted butter, softened
½ cup plus 1 tablespoon powdered sugar
¾ cup all-purpose flour
1 cup quick-cooking oats
½ teaspoon ground cinnamon
4 large eggs
1½ cups granulated sugar
¼ teaspoon salt
1 teaspoon grated lime zest
⅔ cup freshly squeezed lime juice
2 tablespoons milk

1. In a small bowl, combine rum and mint. Set aside.
2. Heat oven to 350°F. Lightly spray a 13-by-9-inch baking pan with cooking spray.
3. In a large bowl, mix butter and ½ cup powdered sugar together with an electric mixer on medium speed. Mix in ½ cup flour, the oats, and cinnamon on low speed, just until well combined. Press into pan. Bake for 22 to 25 minutes, until set and lightly browned. Set aside to cool.

4. Meanwhile, in a large bowl, whisk eggs and granulated sugar. Add remaining ¼ cup flour and salt, whisking until blended. Mix in lime zest, lime juice, and milk.

5. Place a strainer over a medium bowl; pour rum mixture into strainer. Press mixture with the back of a spoon through strainer to drain liquid from leaves; discard leaves. Whisk strained liquid into egg mixture until well combined. Pour over cooled crust. Bake for 25 minutes, or until center is set.

6. Cool completely, about 1 hour. Sift remaining 1 tablespoon powdered sugar over top. Store, covered, in the refrigerator.

Mojito Cake

This recipe makes a beautiful cake or can be converted to cupcakes. For cupcakes, pour batter into green and white papers to keep the mojito theme.

Yield: 12 servings

For cake:
1 box white or yellow cake mix
1 cup club soda
⅓ cup vegetable oil
¼ cup rum
3 tablespoons chopped fresh mint leaves
2 teaspoons grated lime zest
3 large egg whites

For glaze:
½ cup unsalted butter
¼ cup water
1 cup sugar
½ cup rum

For cream cheese icing:
4 ounces unsalted butter, softened
4 ounces cream cheese, softened
2 cups powdered sugar
1 teaspoon pure vanilla extract

Fresh mint leaves
Shredded lime peel

1. Heat oven to 350°F. Line the bottoms of two (9-inch) round cake pans with parchment paper. Lightly grease sides and dust with flour.

2. In a large bowl, beat cake ingredients with an electric mixer on low speed for 30 seconds, then on medium speed for 2 minutes, scraping bowl occasionally. Pour batter into pans. Bake as directed on package for two round pans. Set aside and keep warm.

3. In a 2-quart saucepan, mix glaze ingredients. Bring to a boil over high heat, stirring frequently. Reduce heat to medium; continue to boil for 3 minutes, stirring frequently, until glaze has thickened slightly. Remove cakes from baking pan and place on cooling racks set over a rimmed baking sheet. Poke warm cakes every inch with fork tines. Pour glaze slowly over cakes. Cool cakes completely, about 1 hour.

4. While cakes are cooling, make cream cheese icing. In a large bowl, beat butter and cream cheese together with an electric mixer. With the mixer on low speed, add the powdered sugar 1 cup at a time until smooth and creamy. Beat in the vanilla extract.

5. On a serving plate, place one cake, rounded side down. Frost the top and then add the second layer, rounded side up. Frost with remaining icing. Garnish with mint leaves and lime peel.

Recipe note: For a light meringue frosting, bring 1 cup plus 2 tablespoons sugar, 1½ tablespoons light corn syrup, and 3 tablespoons water to a boil, stirring. Wash down side of pan with a wet pastry brush, and cook the sugar syrup, without stirring, until a candy thermometer registers 230°F. Beat 5 large room-temperature egg whites with a mixer until soft peaks form. Gradually beat in 2 tablespoons sugar. With mixer running, add sugar syrup in a slow, steady stream down side of bowl. Beat on high speed until thick, fluffy, and cool, about 7 minutes. Makes about 6 cups.

Pomegranate Mojito Ice Pops

Taste the liquid mixture as you blend. Homemade pops are easy to make your own by pulling back or adding more sweetener or fruit flavor.

Yield: 4 to 6 servings

⅓ cup freshly squeezed lime juice
¼ cup pomegranate juice
¼ cup sugar, or to taste
2½ cups distilled water
1 teaspoon grated lime zest
2 to 4 pieces julienned fresh mint for each pop
½ to 1 teaspoon pomegranate arils for each pop
Sparkling wine for serving (optional)

1. In a pitcher, combine lime juice and pomegranate juice with sugar, stirring until sugar is completely dissolved. Add distilled water and zest.
2. In the bottom of each ice pop mold, scatter mint and pomegranate arils. Slowly pour in liquid mixture. Top off with a few more arils.
3. Freeze until rock solid. Unmold and serve as is or inverted into glasses of sparkling wine.

Mojito Cheesecake

This simple dessert takes book club or any gathering to a new level. Leftover cake—if there is any—can be stored in the refrigerator for several days.

Yield: 8 to 10 servings

For crust:
2 cups crushed ginger snap cookies
¼ cup unsalted butter, melted

For filling:
3 (8-ounce) packages cream cheese, softened
1 cup sugar
¼ cup light rum
1 tablespoon grated lime zest
2 tablespoons freshly squeezed lime juice
3 large eggs

For topping:
1 cup heavy whipping cream
3 tablespoons powdered sugar
2 teaspoons light rum
2 tablespoons finely chopped fresh mint, plus more whole
   leaves for garnish

1. Heat oven to 350°F. Line the bottom of a nonstick
   9-inch springform pan with parchment paper.

2. In a small bowl, mix crust ingredients. Press into prepared pan. Bake for 8 minutes, or until set. Reduce oven temperature to 300°F. Cool crust completely.

3. For filling, in a large bowl, beat cream cheese, sugar, rum, lime zest, and lime juice with an electric mixer on medium speed. When mixture is fluffy, beat in eggs, one at a time, just until blended. Pour filling over crust.

4. Bake at 300°F for 55 to 65 minutes, until edge of cheesecake is set at least 2 inches from edge of pan but center of cheesecake moves slightly when moved. Turn oven off; open oven door. Let cheesecake remain in oven for 30 minutes. Run a small metal spatula around edge of pan to loosen cheesecake. Cool in pan on a cooling rack for 30 minutes. Refrigerate for at least 6 hours or overnight.

5. For topping, in a chilled bowl, beat cream, powdered sugar, rum, and chopped mint with electric mixer on high speed until soft peaks form.

6. Run a knife around edge of pan and release the pan sides. Invert cake onto a plate, remove bottom plate, and slowly peel off parchment paper. Place a serving plate on top and invert the cake again. Slice and top with whipped cream. Garnish each slice with a mint leaf.

Recipe note: For a fluffier icing, try this meringue spin: Let cheesecake cool in the baking pan. Beat 4 large egg whites and ¼ teaspoon cream of tartar in small bowl with mixer on high speed until foamy. Gradually add ¾ cup extra-fine granulated sugar and 1 tablespoon spiced rum, beating until stiff peaks form. Spoon onto cheesecake. Spread to completely cover top. Bake an additional 8 to 10 minutes, until golden brown. Run knife around rim of pan to loosen cake; cool before removing outside rim. Refrigerate for 4 hours.

Mojito Frozen Custard

Frozen custards are the velvety, ultra-rich members of the ice cream family. Combine two scoops with club soda or lemon-lime soda for a mojito float.

Yield: 1 quart

2 cups heavy cream
1 cup whole milk
¾ cup sugar
1 pinch salt
2 cups loosely packed fresh mint leaves
2 limes, zested
¼ cup rum
3 large egg yolks

1. Place 1 cup cream in a metal bowl sitting over ice.
2. In a saucepan, combine remaining cream, milk, sugar, and salt. Cook over medium heat until sugar is completely dissolved. Stir in mint, lime zest, and rum. Cook until mixture just begins to boil. Immediately take off heat, cover, and set aside for 1 hour.
3. With a fine sieve, strain the infused cream mixture into a bowl. Using a wooden spoon, press down on solids to extract as much flavor as possible. Discard solids and return mixture to saucepan and reheat on medium-low.
4. In a separate bowl, beat the egg yolks. While whisking vigorously, add just a bit of the heated mixture to

temper the yolks. This step keeps you from ending up with scrambled eggs. While continuing to whisk vigorously, poor the tempered egg yolks into the saucepan and continue to stir on medium-low heat. When the mixture is thick enough to cover the back of a spoon, use a fine sieve to strain the mixture into the cream in the ice bath. This will halt the cooking process. When the mixture reaches room temperature, cover the bowl with plastic wrap and refrigerate for 2 hours or up to overnight.

5. Pour the chilled custard into an ice cream maker and process according to the manufacturer's instructions. Freeze overnight.

Mojito Melon Skewers

Desserts don't have to be sugary indulgences. These fruit skewers are light and easy for potlucks, tailgating, or picnics.

Yield: 12 servings

2 limes, zested and juiced
⅓ cup dark rum
3 tablespoons finely chopped fresh mint leaves
5 to 6 cups (1-inch) cubes assorted cantaloupe, honeydew, and watermelon (seedless)
12 (5- to 6-inch) bamboo skewers

1. Combine the rum, lime juice and zest, and mint.
2. Put the melon in a large resealable plastic bag. Pour rum mixture over fruit. Seal bag and gently turn several times to coat fruit without crushing. Refrigerate for 1 hour.
3. Thread 4 or 5 melon cubes onto each skewer and serve.

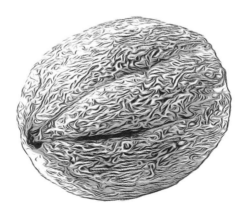

Caramelized Pineapple Mojito Granita

A thin metal baking dish holds the chill nicely while you work the granita into the desired texture. Charring the pineapple brings out its natural sugars.

Yield: 6 servings

4 cups fresh pineapple pieces
¼ cup freshly squeezed lime juice
½ cup distilled water
3 fresh mint leaves, julienned, plus more whole leaves for garnish
6 teaspoons spiced rum

1. In a cast-iron skillet, sear pineapple over high heat for 2 minutes, or until edges turn golden brown and the natural sugars begin to caramelize.
2. Place pineapple in a food processor or blender. Add lime juice and distilled water; pulse just until smooth. Pour into 9-inch square glass or metal baking dish. Stir in mint leaves. Cover; freeze for 30 minutes.

3. With the tines of a fork, scrape the surface to create a textured mixture of large ice crystals. Freeze for 30 minutes more. Scrape mixture again. Repeat until all the mixture resembles snow cone ice. Scoop into dessert dishes or cups. Drizzle each serving with 1 teaspoon rum and garnish with mint.

Mojito Thumbprint Cookies

Add these to your winter and spring holiday cookie platters.

Yield: About 2½ dozen cookies

For cookies:
1½ cups all-purpose flour
¼ teaspoon freshly grated nutmeg
¾ cup unsalted butter, slightly softened
½ cup sugar
2 large eggs, 1 separated
1 teaspoon pure vanilla extract
1¾ cups finely chopped pecans

For mojito filling:
6 tablespoons unsalted butter, softened
1½ cups powdered sugar
1 tablespoon milk
¼ teaspoon spiced rum
⅛ teaspoon grated lime zest
⅛ teaspoon freshly grated nutmeg

1. For the cookies, mix flour and nutmeg in a medium
   bowl. Beat butter and sugar in a large bowl with an
   electric mixer on medium speed until light and fluffy.
   Add 1 whole egg, 1 egg yolk, and vanilla extract; mix
   well. Gradually beat in flour mixture on low speed

until well mixed. Stir in ½ cup nuts. Refrigerate for 30 minutes or until dough is easy to handle.

2. Heat oven to 375°F. Shape dough into 1-inch balls. Roll in egg white then in remaining nuts. Place about 1 inch apart on baking sheets. (Refrigerate remaining dough while baking each batch of cookies.)

3. Bake for 10 minutes or until edges are lightly browned. Remove from oven. Immediately make an indentation in center of each cookie by gently pressing with the back of a small spoon. Cool on baking sheets for 1 minute, then remove to wire racks to cool completely.

4. For the filling, beat butter in a medium bowl until softened. Gradually beat in powdered sugar until fluffy. Beat in milk, rum, lime zest, and nutmeg. Pipe or spoon filling into center of each cooled cookie.

Mojito Icebox Pie

*Icebox pies are a classic southern dessert. They get their
name from the required chilling time in the refrigerator.*

Yield: 9 to 10 servings

2 (14-ounce) cans sweetened condensed milk
6 large egg yolks
1 teaspoon grated lemon zest
1 teaspoon grated lime zest
½ cup freshly squeezed lemon juice
½ cup freshly squeezed lime juice
1 (9-inch) graham cracker crumb crust

For topping:
1 cup heavy whipping cream, chilled
A few drops mint extract
Lemon and lime slices

1. Heat oven to 350°F. Mix condensed milk, egg yolks, lemon
   zest, lime zest, lemon juice, and lime juice until blended.
   Pour into crust.
2. Bake for 20 minutes, or until center is set. Cool completely
   on a cooling rack, about 1 hour. Cover and refrigerate for 4
   hours, or until well chilled.
3. When ready to serve, beat chilled cream in a chilled glass
   bowl. When soft peaks form, drizzle in a few drops of
   mint extract. A little goes a long way, so be cautious about
   additions. Beat cream until stiff peaks form.
4. Garnish pie with minted whipped cream and citrus slices.
   Store covered in refrigerator.

Mojito Milkshakes

Turn this creamy adult libation into shooters for a Fourth of July party or other warm-weather gathering.

Yield: 8 servings

1 teaspoon grated lime zest
2½ tablespoons freshly squeezed lime juice
1 tablespoon spiced rum, plus more for drizzling
4 large mint leaves, plus more for garnish
½ gallon softened vanilla bean ice cream
Milk as needed

1. Puree lime zest, lime juice, rum, and mint leaves in a blender. Fold mixture into softened ice cream. Refreeze ice cream.
2. To prepare each milkshake, blend 1 cup ice cream with ½ cup milk. Pour into a tumbler and garnish with mint and drizzle a little rum on top of each serving.

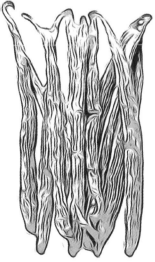

Recipe note: It's often hard to find ½-gallon containers of ice cream in supermarkets. Blue Bell is one manufacturer that still sells them. If you're buying another brand, make sure you can get at least 8 large scoops from the container.

Index

HEATHER MCPHERSON is editor-at-large and columnist for EdibleOrlando. She is a past president of the Association of Food Journalists and is the author of two cookbooks, coauthor of five cookbooks, and editor of three others.